AF269696

Animals In Art

Activity Book

Name: _______________________

Age: _______________________

Class: _______________________

School: _______________________

OXFORD
UNIVERSITY PRESS

Great Clarendon Street, Oxford OX2 6DP

Oxford University Press is a department of the University of Oxford.
It furthers the University's objective of excellence in research, scholarship,
and education by publishing worldwide in

Oxford New York

Auckland Cape Town Dar es Salaam Hong Kong Karachi
Kuala Lumpur Madrid Melbourne Mexico City Nairobi
New Delhi Shanghai Taipei Toronto

With offices in

Argentina Austria Brazil Chile Czech Republic France Greece
Guatemala Hungary Italy Japan Poland Portugal Singapore
South Korea Switzerland Thailand Turkey Ukraine Vietnam

OXFORD and OXFORD ENGLISH are registered trade marks of
Oxford University Press in the UK and in certain other countries

ISBN: 978 0 19 464453 2

Printed in China

This book is printed on paper from certified and well-managed sources.

ACKNOWLEDGEMENTS

Animals in Art Activity Book by: Alistair McCallum

Illustrations by: Kelly Kennedy, Dusan Pavlic/Beehive Illustration,
and Alan Rowe

Introduction Page 3

1 Circle the correct words.

1 A hare looks like a **giraffe** / **rabbit.**

2 A hare can **run** / **fly** fast.

3 An animal's fur is usually **hard** / **soft.**

4 **An artist** / **A photographer** sometimes paints pictures.

5 Most artists can **draw** / **drive** well.

6 The oldest pictures of animals are in **books** / **caves.**

2 Answer the questions.

1 Which animals do you like? (Write two animals.)

____

2 Can you draw or paint?

____

3 Do you have any pets?

____

4 Do you ever take photos of animals, or draw pictures of them?

____

5 Do you know any paintings of animals? What animals are in them?

____

1 Write the words.

  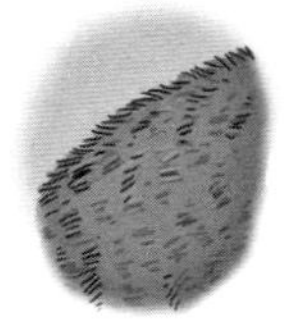

1 p a i n t i n g   2 _ _ _ _   3 _ _ _ _

4 _ _ _ _ _ _ _ _   5 _ _ _ _   6 _ _ _ _ _ _ _

2 Order the words. Then write *true* or *false*.

1 talk. / can / Animals

Animals can talk. ________________________ false

2 from / Animals / people. / different / are

________________________ ____

3 can't / and insects / fly. / birds / Most

________________________ ____

4 born / Florence. / was / Leonardo da Vinci / in

________________________ ____

5 a / Byeon Sang-byeok / artist. / is / Spanish

________________________ ____

1 Write the words.

1 d _esert_ 2 g _________ 3 c _________

4 s _________ 5 b _________ 6 p _________

2 Complete the sentences.

caves   ground   ~~paper~~   plane   paintings
people   animals   walls

1 A long time ago, people had no __paper__ . They painted animals on the _________ of their caves.

2 There are beautiful _________ of giraffes and other animals in some _________ in Libya.

3 About 2,000 years ago, _________ drew giant pictures on the _________ in the Nazca Desert in Peru.

4 You can see amazing pictures of _________ in the Nazca Desert, but you have to be in a _________ .

1 Write the words.

> ocean   stags   mountains   jungle   tigers   desert

1 __________

2 __________

3 __________

4 __________

5 __________

6 __________

2 Write correct sentences.

1 Edwin Landseer was an American artist.

   Edwin Landseer was a British artist.

2 Landseer painted a picture of a tiger.

   ____

3 Stags live in the jungle.

   ____

4 Henri Rousseau was from Brazil.

   ____

5 Rousseau painted a picture of a camel.

   ____

People and Pets ← Pages 10–11

1 Match the parts of sentences.

1 Gold is...   [d]

2 A miniature is...

3 A painting of a person is...

4 A pet is...

5 An emperor is...

6 Jackets and jeans are...

a an animal that lives in your home.

b a very small picture.

c clothes.

d a very expensive metal.

e called a portrait.

f a very important man.

2 Complete the sentences.

1 Francisco de Goya was a <u>S p a n i s h</u> artist. In 1790, he painted a boy and his p _ _ _.

2 A long time ago in India, r _ _ _ people liked h _ _ _ _ _ _ with birds.

3 An artist painted the e _ _ _ _ _ _ Jahangir and his pet f _ _ _ _ _.

1 Write the words.

1 s u e t a t   _statue_

2 r i s p e d   _________

3 u m e m u s   _________

4 p e s u c l u r t   _________

5 m e t t o e l p o   _________

6 o d o w   _________

2 Match. Then write sentences.

People saw a spider	was almost 10 meters high.
Louise Bourgeois	made of wood.
The sculpture	next to a museum.
Native Americans	make tall statues.
They are	called totem poles.
Totem poles are	made a big sculpture.

1 _People saw a spider next to a museum._

2 _________

3 _________

4 _________

5 _________

6 _________

6 Animals in Books ← Pages 14–15

1 Circle and write the correct words.

1 Today, we can __watch__ animals on television.

a (watch)　　　b touch　　　c meet

2 A long time ago, people only looked at drawings of animals __________.

a on the Internet　　b in books　　c on television

3 In *Alice's Adventures in Wonderland,* there are __________ of animals.

a paintings　　　b photos　　　c drawings

4 In the book, a rabbit is __________.

a driving a car　　b wearing clothes
c swimming

5 The drawings in the book are not __________.

a realistic　　　b very nice　　　c in color

2 Complete the sentences.

1 John Audubon was _ _ _ _ in 1785.

2 He _ _ _ _ _ in the USA.

3 He _ _ _ _ lots of birds and other animals.

4 He _ _ _ the drawings in a book.

5 This _ _ _ _ him 20 years.

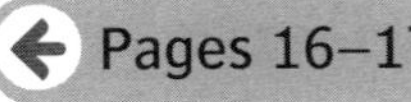 7 Animal Symbols ← Pages 16–17

1 Write the words.

1 $e_r r^o{}_s t^o$ __rooster__

2 $s_e r^o h$ __________

3 $h_e{}^s e p$ __________

4 $k_a{}^s n e$ __________

5 $y_o k{}_m e^n$ __________

6 $t_r i^b a b$ __________

2 Complete the sentences.

> animal   stamps   tiger   France   Korea
> snakes   China   symbol   Egyptian

1 In Ancient __________ writing, there are symbols of animals like birds and __________ .

2 The __________ is the symbol of South __________ , and the rooster is the symbol of __________ .

3 Sometimes you can see an __________ symbol on a country's coins or __________ .

4 In __________ , all the years have an animal __________ .

 Different Animals

1 Order the words.

1 artists / ideas. / Sometimes / different / have

<u>Sometimes artists have different ideas.</u>

2 Animals / are / always / art / realistic. / not / in

____

3 called / stone / used / marble. / a / Brancusi

____

4 a big / table / of / was / stone. / piece / His

____

5 made / pattern. / a nice, / Franz Marc / colored

____

2 Write *Brancusi* or *Franz Marc*.

1 He was an artist from Romania. <u>Brancusi</u>

2 He painted a picture of an elephant, a horse, and a cow. _________

3 He made a sculpture of a seal. _________

4 He was interested in shapes and colors. _________

5 He was a German painter. _________

6 He liked things made of stone. _________

 Teapots and Toys 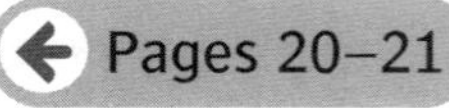

← Pages 20–21

1 Complete the words. Then write the numbers.

1 The horse is a t _o_ _y_. It has wheels. `3`

2 The lion is a sculpture. It is made

   of s __ __ __ __. ☐

3 The t __ __ __ __ __ __ is in the shape of a zebra. ☐

4 The bag is in the s __ __ __ __ of a monkey. ☐

2 Complete the sentences.

artist touch years toys name play sculptures break

1 You can look at __________ of animals in a

   museum, but usually you can't __________ them.

2 When children __________ with toys, they often

   __________ them.

3 About 3,000 __________ ago, an artist made three

   little __________ for children.

4 The __________ lived in Susa. We don't know the

   artist's __________.

1 Write the words.

1 t _ail_   5 b ___________

2 e ___________ 6 h ___________

3 h ___________ 7 m ___________

4 w ___________ 8 c ___________

2 Write correct sentences.

1 Dragons and unicorns are real.

____

2 Dragons have short claws.

____

3 Japanese dragons always have five claws on
each foot.

____

4 A unicorn looks like a white tiger.

____

5 A unicorn has a horn on its back.

____

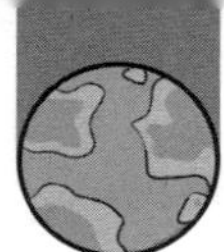

After Reading

1 Check your answers to Activity 1, page 3.

1 = rabbit   2 = run   3 = soft
4 = An artist   5 = draw   6 = caves

2 Complete the puzzle.

3 **Complete. Then find and write the page.**

1 John Audubon drew all the different
  types of <u>b</u> <u>i</u> <u>r</u> <u>d</u> in North America.   <u>page 15</u>

2 There are giant pictures on the ground
  in the Nazca _ _ _ _ _ _ in Peru.   __________

3 Leonardo da _ _ _ _ _ was an
  Italian artist.   __________

4 The oldest paintings are on the
  walls of _ _ _ _ _.   __________

5 The _ _ _ _ _ is the symbol of
  South Korea.   __________

6 A _ _ _ _ _ _ _ _ _ _ is a very
  small picture.   __________

4 **Complete the chart.**

> birds   Louise Bourgeois   ~~sculpture~~   drawing
> Edwin Landseer   ~~seal~~   sculpture   painting

Subject	Type of Art	Artist
<u>seal</u>	<u>sculpture</u>	Constantin Brancusi
stag	__________	__________
spider	__________	__________
__________	__________	John Audubon

My Book Review

Title of this book: _________ __ ____

Name of the author: _________ ____________

This book is about __________ in art.

Questions about this book

1   Write six new words from the book.

____

____

2   What animals are in this book? (Write three animals.)

____

3   Write the names of two artists from the book.

____

What I like about this book

My favorite chapter is ____.

My favorite picture is ____.

My favorite new word is _______________________________________.

My scores for this book (draw ☺, ☺☺, or ☺☺☺)

I like this book. ○○○

I like the pictures. ○○○

I like the picture on the cover. ○○○